# The Gift of Wisdom for Graduates

## 100 wise quotes for 2020 grads

All quotes in the following book are in the public domain.

Introduction, citations, compilation, and design by Logan Thatcher.

# GRADUATE GIFT SERIES

Knowledge without wisdom is trivia

# INTRODUCTION

First things first, congratulations on your achievement. You have, no doubt, acquired a great deal of knowledge, but now it might be a good idea to work on developing some wisdom to make the best use of that knowledge.

As you work your way through the wisdom shared in this text, you might notice some nuggets you like and some you don't. Wisdom isn't always what we'd like it to be. You also might notice some inconsistencies, including many quotes that appear contradictory of one another. This is no accident. One of the most difficult aspects of developing wisdom is understanding that answers aren't always clear. Contradiction isn't always bad. The answer for you might not be the answer for someone else, and making peace with that fact is perhaps the most important aspect of developing wisdom.

Readers might notice that gender pronouns are almost always masculine in these quotes, in addition to the multiple references to "men." We believe these quotes include wisdom applicable to readers regardless of gender, but we felt it would be inappropriate to change gendered quotes out of respect to historical accuracy.

Context is important for everything, and quoting out of context can be dangerous. With this in mind, we painstakingly looked over every quote, and their respective contexts, to make sure we were providing a complete thought applicable to readers, regardless of context, but without in any way misrepresenting the author's original intent.

As always, we welcome all feedback, both in the form of email as well as in reviews on retailer websites, such as Amazon.

### What's the difference between the Cutable and regular editions?

We often hear from readers who enjoy cutting out pages from our books when they find certain quotes particularly inspirational and wish to pin them on a bulletin board or affix them to a refrigerator. But many don't like it when we place quotes on the back pages of other quotes, in the event they'd like to cut out that quote, too. In the Cutable Edition, we've inserted a textless page after every quote, and provided a line where a cutout would best be made for this purpose. The regular edition is presented as we've always done, where all pages provide quotes.

# A wise man will make more opportunities than he finds.

— Sir FRANCIS BACON

# Dangers breed fears, and fears breed more dangers.

— RICHARD BAXTER

Strong towers decay,
But a great name
shall never pass away.

— PARK BENJAMIN

# There is no knowledge which is not valuable.

— EDMOND BURKE

Man has a natural desire to know, One half for interest, the other for show.

— SAMUEL BUTLER

No speech ever
uttered is worth
comparison with
silence.

— THOMAS CARLYLE

# Never make a defense or apology before you are accused.

— *CHARLES I., King of England*

# Be wiser than other people if you can, but do not tell them so.

— EARL OF CHESTERFIELD

Truths turns into dogmas the moment they are disputed.

- G. K. CHESTERTON

# Even the best things, when carried to excess, are wrong.

— Rev. Charles Churchill

Good and bad men
are each less so
than they seem.

— SAMUEL TAYLOR COLERIDGE

# Some men look into everything but see nothing.

— Rev. C. C. COLTON

He who allows
oppression
shares the
crime.

— ERASMUS DARWIN

Men take more pains to lose themselves than would be necessary to keep them on the right road.

— Sir KENELM DIGBY

The only reward of virtue is virtue; the only way to have a friend is to be one.

— Ralph Waldo Emerson

Fools attempt to redeem time's past; Wise live each day as if it were their last.

— WILLIAM DRUMMOND

Man is not the creature of circumstances. Circumstances are the creatures of men.

— BENJAMIN DISRAELI

Don't let us make imaginary evils, when you know we have so many real ones to encounter.

— OLIVER GOLDSMITH

A moment's insight is sometimes worth a life's experience.

— OLIVER WENDELL HOLMES

# There is nothing the body suffers that thesoul may not profit by.

— GEORGE MEREDITH

He who
travels best
knows when
to return
— Thomas Middleton

People are never so
near playing the fool
As when they think
themselves wise.

— *LADY MARY*
*WORTLEY MONTAGU*

# Bliss in possession will not last, Remembered joys are never past.

— JAMES MONTGOMERY

The wrong way always seems the more reasonable.

— GEORGE MOORE

You have not convinced a man because you have silenced him.

— JOHN MORLEY

There is nothing truly
valuable which can
be purchased without
pains and labour.

— *JOSEPH ADDISON*

Where an opinion is general, it is usually correct.

— JANE AUSTEN

Every life, even the most selfish and the most frivolous, is a tragedy at last, because it end with death.

— ALFRED AUSTIN

If a man will begin with certainties, he shall end in doubts; but if he will be content to begin with doubts, he shall end in certainties.

— Sir FRANCIS BACON

**Words, phrases,
fashions pass away;
But truth and nature
live through all.**

— *BERNARD BARTON*

Why slander we the times?
   What crimes
Have days and years, that we
Thus charge them with iniquity?
   If we would rightly scan,
It's not the times are bad, but man.

- DR. J. BEAUMONT

The true standard of equality is seated in the mind; those who think nobly are noble.

— ISAAC BICKERSTAFF

# Mankind will not be reasoned out of the feelings of humanity

— *SIR W. BLACKSTONE*

The man who never
alters his opinion is
like standing water,
breeding reptiles
of the mind.

— WILLIAM BLAKE

Of all the lunacies
earth can boast,
The one that must please
the devils the most
Is pride reduced to
the whimsical terms
Of causing the slugs
to despise the worms.

— *ROBERT BROUGH*

No man can justly censure or condemn another, because indeed no man truly knows another.

— SIR THOMAS BROWNE

As wealth is power,
so all power will
infallibly draw wealth
to itself by some
means or other.

— EDMOND BURKE

# The greatest enemy to man is man.

— *ROBERT BURTON*

For the human heart
is the mirror
Of the things that
are near and far:
Like the wave that
reflects in its bosom
The flower and the
distant star.

— *ALICE CAREY*

**Talk that does not end in any kind of action is better suppressed altogether.**

— *THOMAS CARLYLE*

A young man thinks
an old man is a fool;
But old men know
both men are fools.

— GEORGE CHAPMAN

Advice is seldom welcome; and those who want it the most, always like it the least.

- EARL OF CHESTERFIELD

Where he falls short,
'tis Nature's fault alone;
Where he succeeds,
the merit's all his own.

— Rev. Charles Churchill

# Ambition is the only power that combats love.

— COLLEY CIBBER

That out of sight
is out of mind
Is true of most
we leave behind.

— ARTHUR H. CLOUGH

In life, what begins in fear usually ends in folly.

— SAMUEL TAYLOR COLERIDGE

None are so fond
of secrets as those
who do not mean
to keep them.

— Rev. C. C. COLTON

The wise are too jealous, the fools too secure.

— WILLIAM CONGREVE

# He who quells an angry thought is greater than a king.

## — ELIZA COOK

Thought is deeper
than all speech;
Feeling deeper
than all thought;
Souls to souls
can never teach
What unto themselves
was taught.

— C. P. CRANCH

# Subtlety may deceive you; integrity never will.

— OLIVER CROMWELL

# Men of quality are above wit.

— JOHN CROWNE

Of all bad things
by which mankind
are cursed,
Their own bad
tempers surely
are the worst.

— *RICHARD CUMBERLAND*

Self-destruction is the effect of cowardice in the highest extreme.

— DANIEL DE FOE

# Variety is the mother of enjoyment.
## — BENJAMIN DISRAELI

Good actions still must be maintained with As bodies nourished with resembling food.

— *JOHN DRYDEN*

# The use of history is to give value to the present hour and its duty.

— Ralph Waldo Emerson

# Revenge is profitable, gratitude is expensive.
## — EDWARD GIBBON

# There is no vulture like despair.

## — GEORGE GRANVILLE

It is the folly of the world constantly which confounds its wisdom.

— OLIVER WENDELL HOLMES

To live long is almost everyone's wish but to live well is the ambition of a few.

— JOHN HUGHES

# Irrationally held truths may be more harmful than reasoned errors.

— THOMAS HENRY HUXLEY

# Happy is the man who hath never known the taste of fame.

— SIR EDWARD GEORGE EARLE LYTTON

Politeness has been well defined as benevolence in small things.

- THOS. BABINGTON MACAULAY

An innocent truth can never stand in need of a guilty lie.

— PHILIP MASSINGER

# Absence not long enough to root out all love, increases love at second sight.

— *THOMAS MAY*

# Observation is the most enduring of the pleasures of life.

— *GEORGE MEREDITH*

# Great talkers are never great doers.

## — Thomas Middleton

Politeness costs nothing and gains everything.

— Lady Mary Wortley Montagu

A day in such serene enjoyment spent Is worth an age of splendid discontent.

— JAMES MONTGOMERY

The man who loses
his opportunity,
loses himself.

— George Moore

# Small habits well pursued at times May reach the dignity of crimes

— Hannah More

It is not enough
to do good; one
must do it in a
good way.

— John Morley

'Tis better to love and be poor, than be rich with an empty heart.

— Sir Lewis Morris

There is in human nature, generally, more of the fool than of the wise.

- Sir FRANCIS BACON

Who never doubted,
never half believed.

— PHILIP J. BAILEY

It is a general popular error to suppose the loudest complainers for the public to be the most anxious for its welfare.

— *EDMOND BURKE*

**Self-contemplation is infallibly the symptom of disease, be it or be it not the cure.**

— THOMAS CARLYLE

An injury is much sooner forgotten than an insult.

– EARL OF CHESTERFIELD

# Fame
# Is nothing
# but an empty
# name.

— Rev. Charles Churchill

What we all love
is good touched
up with evil;
Religion's self must
have a spice of devil.

— ARTHUR H. CLOUGH

# There is moderation even in excess.

## — BENJAMIN DISRAELI

To be conscious that you are ignorant is a great step to knowledge.

— BENJAMIN DISRAELI

Write it on your heart
that every day is the
best day of the year.

— Ralph Waldo Emerson

# There is no heaven like mutual love.

— GEORGE GRANVILLE

# Life is a great bundle of little things.

— OLIVER WENDELL HOLMES

If a little knowledge is dangerous, where is the man who has so much as to be out of danger?

— THOMAS HENRY HUXLEY

# There are a thousand doors to let out life.

— PHILIP MASSINGER

# When passion only speaks, Truth is not always there

— *Thomas Middleton*

# Life is too short for any distant aim; And cold the dull reward of future fame.

— Lady Mary Wortley Montagu

To joys to exquisite to last,
And yet more exquisite
when past.

— JAMES MONTGOMERY

The difficulty in life
is the choice.

— George Moore

A great interpreter
of life ought not be
the one who needs
interpretation.

— John Morley

It is a strange desire, to seek power, and to lose liberty.

— Sir FRANCIS BACON

The concessions of the weak are the concessions of fear.

- EDMOND BURKE

A loving heart is
the beginning of
all knowledge.

— THOMAS CARLYLE

# There is no wisdom like frankness.

— *BENJAMIN DISRAELI*

To be great
is to be
misunderstood.

— *Ralph Waldo Emerson*

# General notions are generally wrong.

— *Lady Mary Wortley Montagu*

The great business of life is to be, to do, to do without, and to depart.

— John Morley

# Citations in order of appearance

SIR FRANCIS BACON (1560-1626).
From Essays of Ceremonies and Respects

RICHARD BAXTER (1615-1691).
From Hypocrisy

PARK BENJAMIN (1809-1861).
From A Great Name.

EDMOND BURKE (1730-1797).
From Speech on American Taxation

SAMUEL BUTLER (1612-1680).
Former Satire–Human Learning

THOMAS CARLYLE (1795--1881).
Lectures (1838)

CHARLES I., King of England (1600-1649).
From Letter to Lord Wentworth.

EARL OF CHESTERFIELD (1694-1773).
From Letter to his Son

G. K. CHESTERTON (1874-1936).
From Heretics

REV. CHARLES CHURCHILL (1731-1764).
From The Apology

SAMUEL TAYLOR COLERIDGE (1772-1834).
April 19, 1830.

Rev. C. C. COLTON (1780-1832).
From Lacon.

ERASMUS DARWIN (1731-1802).
From The Botanic Garden

Sir KENELM DIGBY (1603-1665).
From The Broad Stone of Honor

BENJAMIN DISRAELI (1804-1881).
From Vivian Grey

WILLIAM DRUMMOND (1585-1649).
Flowers of Sin.

RALPH WALDO EMERSON (1803-1882).
From Essays

OLIVER GOLDSMITH (1728-1774).
From The Good Natured Man

OLIVER WENDELL HOLMES (1809-1894).
From The Poet at the Breakfast Table.

GEORGE MEREDITH (1828-1909).
From Diana of the Crossways

THOMAS MIDDLETON (1570-1627).
From The Old Law

LADY MARY WORTLEY MONTAGU (1690-1762).
From Letter to Lady Bute

JAMES MONTGOMERY (1771-1854).
From The Pelican Island

GEORGE MOORE (1855-1933).
From The Bending of the Bough

JOHN MORLEY (1838-1923).
From Life of Gladstone

JOSEPH ADDISON (1672-1719).
From The Tatler. No. 97

JANE AUSTEN (1775-1817).
From Mansfield Park.

ALFRED AUSTIN (1835-1913).
From Savonarola.

SIR FRANCIS BACON (1560-1626).
From Proficience and Advancement of Learning,

—BERNARD BARTON (1784-1849).
From Stanzas on Bloomfield.

DR. J. BEAUMONT (1616-1699).
From Original Poems.

ISAAC BICKERSTAFF (e. 1735-1787).
From The Maid of the Mill

SIR W. BLACKSTONE (1723- 1780).
From Commentaries. 1, 5.

WILLIAM BLAKE (1757- 1827).
From Marriage of Heaven and Hell.

ROBERT BROUGH (1828-1860).
From The Tentmaker's Story.

SIR THOMAS BROWNE (1605-1682)
From Religio Medici

EDMOND BURKE (1730-1797).
From Speech on the Economic Reform

ROBERT BURTON (1576-1640).
From Anatomy or Melancholy.

ALICE CAREY (1820-1871).
From The Time to be

THOMAS CARLYLE (1795--1881).
From Inaugural Lecture at Edinburgh.

GEORGE CHAPMAN (1559-1634).
From All Fools

EARL OF CHESTERFIELD (1694-1773).
From Letter to his Son

REV. CHARLES CHURCHILL (1731-1764).
From The Apology

COLLEY CIBBER (1671-1757).
from Caesar in Egypt

ARTHUR H. CLOUGH (1819-1861).
From Songs of Absence

SAMUEL TAYLOR COLERIDGE (1772-1834).
Oct. 5, 1830.

REV. C. C. COLTON (1780-1832).
From Lacon.

WILLIAM CONGREVE (1670-1728).
From The Way of the World

ELIZA COOK (1818-1889).
From Anger.

C. P. CRANCH (1813-1892).
From Stanzas

OLIVER CROMWELL (1599-1658).
From Letters.

JOHN CROWNE (1650-1703).
From Sir Courtly Nice

RICHARD CUMBERLAND (1732-1811),
From Menander.

DANIEL DE FOE (1661-1731).
From The History of Projects

BENJAMIN DISRAELI (1804-1881).
From Vivian Grey

JOHN DRYDEN (1631-1700).
From Satire of the Dutch

RALPH WALDO EMERSON (1803-1882)
From Society and Solitude

EDWARD GIBBON (1737-1794).
From Decline and Fall of the Roman Empire.

GEORGE GRANVILLE (1667-1735).
From Peleus and Thetis

OLIVER WENDELL HOLMES (1809-1894).
From The Professor at the Breakfast Table.

JOHN HUGHES (1677-1720).
From The Lay Monastery

THOMAS HENRY HUXLEY (1825-1895).
From Science and Culture

EDWARD GEORGE EARLE LYTTON (1805-1873).
From Last of the Barons

THOS. BABINGTON MACAULAY (1800-1859).
from Boswell's Life of Johnson

PHILIP MASSINGER (1584-1639).
From The Emperor or the East.

THOMAS MAY (1595-1650).
From Henry II

GEORGE MEREDITH (1828-1909).
From Diana of the Crossways

THOMAS MIDDLETON (1570-1627).
From Blurt, Master-Constable

LADY MARY WORTLEY MONTAGU (1690-1762).
From Letters

JAMES MONTGOMERY (1771-1854).
From Greenland

GEORGE MOORE (1855-1933).
From The Bending of the Bough

HANNAH MORE (1744-1833).
From Sensibility

JOHN MORLEY (1838-1923).
From On Compromise

SIR LEWIS MORRIS (1833-1907).
From Love in Death

SIR FRANCIS BACON (1560-1626).
From Essays of Boldness

PHILIP J. BAILEY (1816-1901).
From Festus.

EDMOND BURKE (1730-1797).
From Observations of a Publication

THOMAS CARLYLE (1795--1881).
From Characteristics

EARL OF CHESTERFIELD (1694-1773).
From Letter to his Son

REV. CHARLES CHURCHILL (1731-1764).
From The Ghost

ARTHUR H. CLOUGH (1819-1861).
From Dipsychus

BENJAMIN DISRAELI (1804-1881).
From Vivian Grey

BENJAMIN DISRAELI (1804-1881).
From Popanilla

RALPH WALDO EMERSON (1803-1882).
From Society and Solitude

GEORGE GRANVILLE (1667-1735).
From Peleus and Thetis

OLIVER WENDELL HOLMES (1809-1894).
From The Poet at the Breakfast Table.

THOMAS HENRY HUXLEY (1825-1895).
From Science and Culture

PHILIP MASSINGER (1584-1639).
From Parliament of Love

THOMAS MIDDLETON (1570-1627).
From The Old Law

LADY MARY WORTLEY MONTAGU (1690-1762).
From Epistle to the Earl of Burlington

JAMES MONTGOMERY (1771-1854).
From The Pelican Island

GEORGE MOORE (1855-1933).
From The Bending of the Bough

JOHN MORLEY (1838-1923).
From Miscellanies

SIR FRANCIS BACON (1560-1626).
From Essays of Great Place

We hope you've enjoyed your copy of The Gift of Wisdom for Graduates. We sincerely want to congratulate you on the monumental achievement of your graduation. Hopefully this book has been a small part of your lifelong education.

GOOD GIFT
Books

# If you enjoyed The Gift of Wisdom, you might like The Gift of Adulting.

Cutable and regular editions available on Amazon

〉〈 GOOD GIFT 〉〈
Books

2019 GRADUATE EDITION

## The Gift of ADULTING for Graduates

100 scriptures about personal responsibility

Made in the USA
Coppell, TX
31 May 2020